GENIUS LOCI

D1602569

Also by Alison Hawthorne Deming

Poetry

The Monarchs: A Poem Sequence
Science and Other Poems
Poetry of the American West (editor)

Nonfiction

Writing the Sacred into the Real
The Edges of the Civilized World: A Journey
in Nature and Culture
Temporary Homelands
Girls in the Jungle
The Colors of Nature (coeditor)

GENIUS LOCI

ALISON HAWTHORNE DEMING

PENGUIN POETS

PENGUIN BOOKS
Published by the Penguin Group
Penguin Group (USA) Inc., 375 Hudson Street, New York, New York 10014, U.S.A.
Penguin Group (Canada), 10 Alcorn Avenue, Toronto, Ontario, Canada M4V 3B2 (a division of
Pearson Penguin Canada Inc.)
Penguin Books Ltd, 80 Strand, London WC2R 0RL, England
Penguin Ireland, 25 St Stephen's Green, Dublin 2, Ireland (a division of Penguin Books Ltd)
Penguin Group (Australia), 250 Camberwell Road, Camberwell, Victoria 3124, Australia
(a division of Pearson Australia Group Pty Ltd)
Penguin Books India Pvt Ltd, 11 Community Centre, Panchsheel Park, New Delhi–110 017, India
Penguin Group (NZ), cnr Airborne and Rosedale Roads, Albany, Auckland 1310, New Zealand
(a division of Pearson New Zealand Ltd)
Penguin Books (South Africa) (Pty) Ltd, 24 Sturdee Avenue, Rosebank, Johannesburg 2196,
South Africa

Penguin Books Ltd, Registered Offices:
80 Strand, London WC2R 0RL, England

First published in Penguin Books 2005

1   3   5   7   9   10   8   6   4   2

Page vii constitutes an extension of this copyright page.

LIBRARY OF CONGRESS CATALOGING IN PUBLICATION DATA
Deming, Alison Hawthorne, 1946–
Genius loci / Alison Hawthorne Deming.
p.   cm.
ISBN 0-14-303520-7
I. Title.
PS3554.E474G46 2005
811'.54—dc22   2004065313

Printed in the United States of America
Set in Janson Text
Designed by Ginger Legato

for malcolm

ACKNOWLEDGMENTS

Grateful acknowledgment is given to the following journals in which these poems appeared: *Alaska Quarterly Review:* "The Naturalists," "Wild Fruit"; *Hawaii Review:* "Arboretum," "La Paz"; *Hayden's Ferry Review:* "Making Love to You When You're Far Away," "The List"; *Hunger Mountain Review:* "Matins for Andre Dubus"; *Maize:* "Union Square," "New Shoes, 1939"; *Nebraska Review:* "Learning Again to Love"; *North Dakota Review:* "The Old Man"; *Orion:* "Short Treatise on Birds"; *Oriononline:* "Rehearsal Space for War"; *Painted Bride Quarterly:* "The Blackwater"; *Rio Grande Review:* "For the Thief"; *Southwestern American Literature:* "Driving through Nature," "The Rock Fig"; *Spork:* "The Changing Place," "The Charting"; *Water~Stone:* "Wild Woman of the Woods"; *Whole Terrain:* "On Sagadahoc Bay," "Under the Influence of Ironwoods"; *Wild Duck Review:* "The Phenomenology of Shopping," "In Spring: Drift Creek"; *Wilderness:* "The Enigma We Answer by Living."

These poems appeared in the following anthologies:

"Arboretum"
Like Thunder: Poets Respond to Violence in America, ed. Virgil Suarez and Ryan G. Van Cleave (Iowa City: University of Iowa Press, 2002)

"The Yaak"
The Roadless Yaak, ed. Rick Bass (Guilford, Conn.: Lyons Press, 2002)

"Driving through Nature," "The Rock Fig"
Getting Over the Color Green: Contemporary Environmental Literature of the Southwest, ed. Scott Slovic (Tucson: University of Arizona Press, 2001)

"Biophilia," "God"
Poets of the New Century, ed. Roger Weingarten and Richard Higgerson (Jaffrey, N.H.: David R. Godine, 2001)

I am grateful to the Djerassi Resident Artists Program, Mesa Refuge, the Sitka Center for Art and Ecology, and the University of Arizona for gifts of time that furthered this work. The title poem was inspired by time spent in the Czech Republic teaching at the Prague Summer Seminars, for which I thank Richard Katrovas. The Orion Society has, over the past decade, provided fellowship with like-minded writers for whom artistic and activist impulses share a common source, and this work is a small payment toward my many debts of gratitude.

CONTENTS

. . . there is no explaining
the dark it is only the light
that we keep feeling a need to account for

—W. S. Merwin

GENIUS LOCI

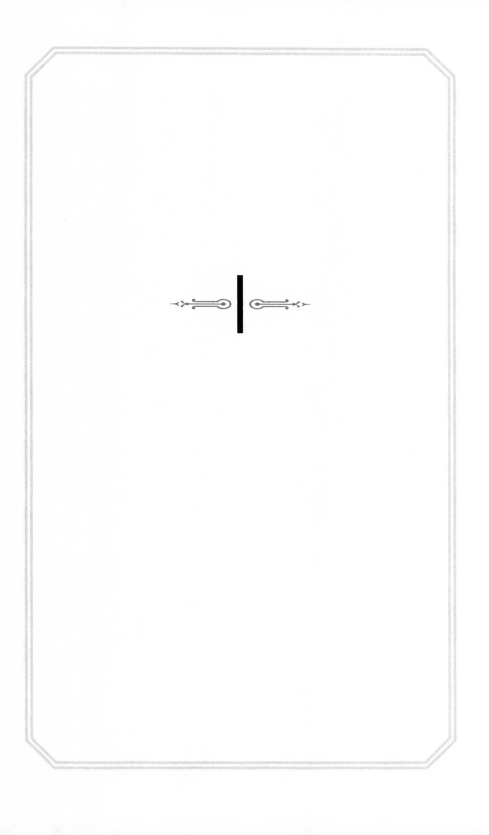

THE NATURALISTS

When the naturalists
see a pile of scat,
they speed toward it
as if a rare orchid
bloomed in their path.
They pick apart
the desiccated turds,
retrieving a coarse
black javelina hair
or husk of piñon nut
as if unearthing gems.
They get down on their knees
to nose into flowers
a micron wide—belly flowers,
they say, because that's
what you get down on
to see them. Biscuitroot,
buffalo gourd, cryptogams
to them are hints of
some genetic memory
fossilized in their brains,
an ancient music they try
to recall because,
although they can't quite
hear the tune, they know
if they could sing it
that even their own wild
rage and lust and death
terrors would seem
as beautiful as the
endolithic algae
that releases nitrogen
into rocks so that
junipers can milk them.

—for Gary Paul Nabhan

THE YAAK

1

At the party in Missoula everyone
was excited about the poetry slam
in Troy. I said I'm going north
to take a walk in the woods with
Rick Bass, and all they could talk
about was how last year Denis Johnson
lit his book on fire after reading
from it. I said I'm going north
to take a walk with Rick Bass,
then someone heard me and asked,
You're going to the Yaak? (like it's
a god not a place which it is) that's not
the middle of nowhere, it's beyond it,
the edge.

                    I drove
the Clark Fork, road that follows
water's lead, up out of plains
and hills to the thick place
where mountain and river
and forest work together without
interference until the scabs
of harvesting come. Still
ravines of blue-green darkness called,
larch and hemlock, and the hand-drawn
map took me into them, then
grizzly country, ice layered
blue on Hell Roaring Creek.

                    When I arrived
Lowry barefoot on the porch—She's
driving a silver limo!—the celebrity of
any visitor coming to the far away.
Mary Catherine—was she reading,
painting, something inward? Rick
planting bulbs in the near-frozen

ground. Elizabeth heating soup.
First walk—I'm not afraid of
bears, she said, but the lions
will stalk you. One walked
right by that window. Last
winter, here, near the cabin made
of the homestead's salvaged beams,
I saw two black bear cubs. Here
a pack of wolves—usually it's
only one. Here,
he said

      (what they've witnessed
of the untamed world marking
their landscape like
animal scent), under a tree
like this (big larch with
yellow rain of needles
spilled like sawdust—
I thought at first
it was the work of
woodpeckers drilling and
leaving a mess behind—
but, no, then the fallen
needles looked like light
the tree had spilled,
a halo on the ground),

in a place like this, he said,
sheltered and dry, in winter
you might see five or six deer
lined up, stores, left by
a lion—and then more larches,
a few giant elders, others
reaching the age when
bark is thick enough
to outlast a fire, and then
the spot where wildfire bloomed
and they came with buckets, the
girls with watering cans, for days,

and long after they thought
the fire was out, night after night,
the ground glowed red.

2

In the dark before sunrise
we eat cheese toast and dress
so thick we walk like moonmen
across the crusted marsh
and into the sleeping woods. Yesterday
tracks in snow—a very big animal,
they'd said, bending down to see,
urine spattered, buck sign on
three trees marking trail
where the does pass,
buck's arousal scraped into wood,
saplings bark-bare and raw
where he rubbed and rubbed his scent.

Rick's set up out of sight, my job
to lie beneath a giant larch,
await the light, rattle antlers
and grunt the buck's call,
riling the old stag to defend
his dominion.

On ground
hallowed by scat and spit
and pillage of wolf, bear, and lion,
stories now are prey—one hunter
found two skeletons, antlers
deadlocked, bucks fixed in
combat's embrace then
the shared quiet end, though
each must have cried out
against its helplessness;
another hunter—tone of voice
the mark of his aroused

admiration—watched a buck
work a circle of five does,
moving from one to the other,
mounting and jerking
until he'd had them all.

                    3

              I love to think
my animal presence
is equal to being
predator or prey, no agent
only of dominion, rather
subject to the rule
of violent need—all I might
inflict might be inflicted
on me. But truth is harder
than desire. The human mind
makes seeds that spew and drift
and carry us far from will
or wish to be benign. Most of what
we generate floats
through neurological space,
making us confuse what
we dream with how we live.

It's time to leave the forest,
go home for pancakes and coffee,
and let the ravens and squirrels
move on to smaller complaints.
We creak up out of hiding,
our footsteps loud, stopping
the snowshoe rabbit that freezes
on the haunch of a snowy deadfall.
Pure white, except the godly
brown ears, it watches us, thinking
nothing that my human mind
can comprehend—not, Should I
escape, or, Am I hiding well enough,

or Great-Force-of-Mystery
protect me. It just thinks
the stillness its body demands.

—for Rick Bass

THE BLACKWATER

Traveling past deadfall hickory
and cypress knees, past the
pearly eggs of apple snails
beaded onto pickerelweed,
metallic lace the golden orb spiders
had strung between us and the sky,
we paddled where the river
took us, easy bending
passage through a wilderness
that gave way enough only
for us to keep moving, unsure
where we'd come ashore
or turn back to pull upstream
and home. Oh, but it was
peaceful, riding like flotsam
on the current, silently
scaring off the gator,
buzzard and hawk that
knew us even in
our gentleness as danger.
One glistening anhinga
noticed us so late it
stood frozen on a snag,
our plastic hulls nosing up
so close we felt at last harmless.

Cool amber dark moving element,
musk of peat, silt and root gnarl
suspended in its tannin tea—
why should I feel at home
in its tireless flowing, as if I'd
never left the amnion where
spirit first meets flesh, as if
I could remember what
lies ahead where
molecules disperse to seed
the sea. On the river
not knowing what's ahead

is what moves us forward—
one more oxbow, we think,
stroking our blades into
resinous riffle and pool, all
the while knowing
we'll never be more
complete than this, never
appetite more quiet than
gliding through the
sword-shadow of sabal
palm and saw palmetto.

—after Elizabeth Bishop

NEAR ZION

Two ravens landed
on a lean piñon
and perched alert to
the blue day staring
as if to think then
the female grooming
herself then the male.
He cawed head reaching
shoulders lifting wings
from their tight folds the
feathers black satin
like the sheen of pelt.
He tilted his head
up and aside first
left then right raising
one eye to the sky.
Was it a question
or hunger or stiff
neck that made him stretch?
The two birds so calm
there atop the time-
scoured banded stone.
And I saw us side
by side content in
the moment, aware
of the scale that houses
and diminishes
us—then they flew off.

—for Malcolm

THE TEMPLE HARLOT

Tell him about the power of the wild man.
Ask him to send a harlot back with you,
A temple prostitute, to conquer him
With her greater power.

—*Gilgamesh*, TRANSLATED BY DAVID FERRY

What was the problem for which she was the solution?
A hairy-bodied man unset the traps and the creatures got free.

How did she lure him away from his mission?
She visited the watering place and showed him her beauty.

Why did the animals flee from him then?
He was no longer an animal. He was now as beautiful as a god.

When he lay down on her was it then that his understanding began?
No. Then he lost himself in her. Later when the animals fled he knew.

What did he know then the wild man who had grazed with the gazelles?
He knew he was no longer a wild man. His body was no longer able to
    follow the beasts.

If she was a harlot why did she live in the temple?
Because though her work is sacred the wild man must pay to lie with her.

How can the woman's work be sacred when the man
no longer can drink with the beasts whose hearts delight in water?
The woman's work is sacred because when he lay with her
the wild man's mind ran with the beasts.

Why was the harlot reviled and made to drink what flows in alley gutters?
Because she was the portal through which he entered his destiny.

What is the wild man's destiny?
To sit in the house of the dead among the shadow companions.

What convinced the wild man not to revile her?
That she was the portal through which he entered his destiny.

What is the wild man's destiny?
To be remembered by those who love him.

Where is the harlot today?
Homeless, giving shelter in her rags to strays.

WILD WOMAN OF THE WOODS

First I let the vines grow over my door,
stopped opening the suitcase full of lies,
progress in a thousand glossy shades
of appetite, making me think, I need
this need, always the fiction the body writes,
always the need finding an address in the flesh,
driving me through the city like a whale
through krill. I wandered, spending more and more
time in the woods, where hunger was real, chance
protecting some lives and turning some to food.
I wanted to be no more safe, no more
damaging, than creatures, to be their equal.

                          I gave up
cutting back on green's profusion, wanted
to be in beauty and of it, to be lush and bend
like wood around a wound or obstacle
as ancient trees take into their flesh the slash
of lightning strike, the bullet's sudden insult
or barbed wire's slow one, violence subsumed
in growth, an incident in an otherwise metabolically
balanced life.

                 Once, in that other life, houseled and clean,
I read that whales in their evolutionary history had been
terrestrial but changed to live in the sea because
that's what life asked of them. I'm not sure
what life is asking of me. I hear the house-happy
women whisper and jeer. She will steal
your children and eat them for supper—look how
the wind whistles through her lips, her hair
a nest for spiders—she will steal your soul and
make you wild.

                 I'm not sure what it means to lose
your way home and start seeing the wild as a force
that can enter at will and remake you, life,
what Earth does through you, and it can change

its mind any day. Yes, I was lonely, hungry and cold.
I slept on dried moss and pine needles, making
what bedding and bowls I needed when I needed them
and leaving them behind when I did not. What days
meant to me were joy and grief—watching a guileless rabbit
nibble on grass, then piercing it for roasting.
I wept watching flocks of starlings whirl,
herds of elk feed upon the grasslands,
communal bats spilling from caves at dusk
to feed on insects riding the aeolian,
but when I came alone to the watering places
the creatures fled, knowing I was not their kin.

Some nights I crept near parking lots bordering
malls and movies, crouched in leafy cover
to eavesdrop on couples whose conversation
was so casual, as if it were nothing
for one to say to another, "Well, what
do you think of that?" Or for a man, thinking
no one was watching, furtive and fast as a rat,
to press a woman against the side of his car.
I could have been as sure with my need, if
I had believed it would do no harm.

                              My idea
of wildness became more quiet, encompassing
the forest's slow-growing entanglements, no longer
mustangs, cougars and bears, but wild oaks,
wolf lichen and moss, the ground in process
of penetration and repair. After I memorized
the paths of a hundred stars, dying was easy,
like becoming diluted in forest mist. One day
I got lost in a fog so thick I could no longer tell
where my body ended and the space surrounding it began.

MATINS FOR ANDRE DUBUS

We knocked on your door that afternoon
while you were making love, apparent
when you answered, zipping up, laughing,
the joyful exertion like sunburn on your face.

Then like a noisy pack of dogs we hit
Commercial Street heading for Napi's
where you treated the whole round table
of poets to oysters and beer. This was before

you were stricken. You could still walk—
two knees to hold you in lovemaking
and prayer, both of which you savored the way
God must savor the wholeness of contradiction.

This morning sitting alone I remember
your story about the father who must choose
whether to do what's right or to harbor
his daughter who's done wrong, a man

of faith who must harbor himself, accepting
what the world inflicts as a lesson
without expecting a cure. Andre,
I am still here where your suffering weighs

the same as your joy, and the world goes on
asking for what's impossible, and the only choice
is to give it, as the faithful give themselves
to God to prevent being taken by faithlessness.

GOD

God was bored with everything
being the same and so
He created difference, everything
cracking, splitting, splaying,
crumbling, and God said,
It is good, a planet that splinters
into light. My animal, God said,
comes when I call, my animal
speaks to me when hungry,
my animal sleeps off the kill,
licks what tastes strong, takes love
when it's there, and God said,
It is good, progress, the plane gone down
in the enemy's forest, two armies,
one bent on murder and one
bent on grace, racing toward
the collision where the pilot lies
wounded. God wonders how
to be gentle with His dominance,
the late paradise a ruin, golden
monkeys and rats snacking and
leaving their stains in the sanctuary,
and God says, It is good, the galaxy
spinning like water down a drain,
difference longing for sameness and
killing itself to get there. There
you are, says God, arms opening,
I missed you. And all of it is so good,
the universe of hydrogen and eyes,
engines, hunger and prophylactic pain.

FOR THE THIEF

Thank you for leaving the desk and the chair,
the books, snapshots and piano.
I've heard of moving van robberies—
coming home from work to percussion
of empty rooms. Thank you for
leaving the trapped air
that softens the blunt edge of my day.
What's mine—the hum of identity—
still surrounds me,
though the electronics
are gone and the jewelry
that was too precious to wear.
Thank you for not spraying
the walls with coke or with piss.
Thank you for being a professional,
tidy and quick, entering with a clean
silent cut, not wasting your time
or mine with vandalism or assault.
When my mother was robbed
the closets and drawers were dumped
on the floor. All that was stolen were
towels that had hung in her bathroom.
Her neighbors, the police said, had
lost their cookware. Better our houses
become someone's mall than shooting range.
With my cousins, one in New York took
a knife-blade against her throat.
Another in Madrid was dragged
three blocks by her hair. Thank you
for knowing what you were here for,
for tending to your business without rage.

ARBORETUM

Walking to cure myself of the gun proud
cabbie who brought me here—azalea,
camellias, pink rhododendron, falling
in a storm of flowers—the government,
his enemy, to blame for lack of morals,
parents arrested, guns taken if they
discipline their children—I find
a Japanese cherry in full bloom
though its foot thick trunk is scarred
with a healing gash that spirals
from the ground up the bark to
where the wood narrows branching
to waterfall over my head.
Of the human and infant rubble
fallen in Oklahoma City he bemoaned only
what he called the government's
latest scapegoat and considered
what he'd do if agents came
to the door to take his guns—
better to run than fight so they wouldn't
kill his wife and child he guessed.
Should I fear him or what he fears?
He's the one who says he'd
do something about it if he saw
a woman raped—not like those
New Yorkers, a dozen staring,
getting off or too scared to act.
Should I fear him or the ones
he fears—eight black guys stopped his cab.
If it weren't for this gun—it was tucked,
then I knew it, under his seat—
I'd be dead now. Should I fear him
or the one he fears, I who believe,
little do-gooder, daydreamer, girlscout,
that we should have no guns, no sovereign states,

no infidelity, no greed. I'm the only woman
walking here alone under the crowned trees.
Rich houses on the hill across the street
train their glass eyes on a distant flowering.

UNDER THE INFLUENCE OF IRONWOODS

Sunrise. Yesterday's dust storm spun thin soil from fallow cotton fields. The air today disturbed, sun seeping through milky clouds like butter melting in oatmeal.

Dirt road grids through creosote scrub. Pump Station Road. Silverbell Road. Tailings pond. Bullet holes lace the yellow road sign, fat black steer, hindquarters punched with daylight.

The road reddens—iron bleeding from the mountains. Saguaros grow dense—standing sentinel for the unpeopled place. Flicker, thrasher, gnat-catcher, elf owl, cactus wren, inca dove, kingbird, titmouse, jackrabbit, bobcat, packrat, pocket gopher, pocket mouse, peccary, kit fox, coyote, leaf-nosed bat, free-tail bat, sharp-shinned hawk, zone-tailed hawk, whip-tail, skink, spadefoot, chuckwalla, vine snake, gopher snake, coachwhip, sidewinder, diamondback, turkey vulture, mule deer, swift.

And the ironwoods, so quiet, if we had not read their primer we would not see the blue-green haze of their nurture, each one a tangled mess of life—trellising vines, nesting doves, roosting hawks, climbing squirrels, the rain of seeds falling and nestling into leaf thickened ground, nursery of wild-flowers and cacti under its shade, burrow of desert tortoise among its roots, confusion of microlives in the soil.

Ragged Top gouges the sky, serrated blade of quaternary rock. Below—paloverde, cholla, greasewood, so lush the ironwoods are lost to us. An eight-hundred-year-old ought to stand up and announce itself. But none do. They are all about relationship not size. We clump up the wash—maybe this? maybe this? lifting the downed limbs to test their weight. Ironwood so heavy it will sink in water, dull tools, its deadwood last a thousand years.

We climb upslope. Below us wildness stretches across the range until mountains break the view. No sign of human work or habitation. Not a jet or contrail in the sky. Just the purposeful bird-riddled blanket of green.

No, not a blanket, but a sea, where land has settled down after long up-heaval, and softer mountains cruise like ships—there's a little dory to the north, a massive battleship to the west, and a cluttered regatta of sailboats to the northeast. The quiet sea, life swimming over the land, the thickening of the green world into every crevice that will harbor the least of it. Washed up at my feet, one yellow poppy, small and bright as a dime.

We keep climbing, our goal, the narrow northwest saddle. We billygoat up through scattered pink cactus flowers and glowing cholla, my companion leading over the scree and I following, learning every variety of thorn and spine so that when we reach the stony platform of the summit, I boast the mark of untamed land along my bare arms like the scratches of a bobcat.

High under the outleaning cliff lies an oval of hard dirt, stones kicked aside, dried pellets of scat, where a mule deer (or bighorn?) lies down, this quiet not exceptional to the creature, this vastness his home, where he rests and grinds his jaw and stares into light to think.

Below, the seam of flowering yellow paloverde explains the path that water takes across the arid land.

There is an explanation for everything except beauty. Why should I be a mechanism that registers beauty? Why should I need the beauty of that golden lichen thriving on a south facing rock, that saguaro adding mid-column a new wedged rib of flesh, that fairy duster blooming with a scent like cotton candy mixed with semen, that rock extruded from the earth's belly basking now among the living, that ironwood so conservation minded for centuries it never overspends the budget imposed by arid land?

I was born to love this world, to find what binds me to the long history of life on Earth, to name the places where natural beauty quiets the overburden of living, to study form as it invents and reinvents itself in the things of the world, to cry out against the diminishment of nature's god-wild complexity, and to praise the singular wild poppy as if it were the first or the last one on Earth. Under the influence of ironwoods, I understand that to nurture is to live.

—written in support of the Ironwood National Monument

THE ENIGMA WE ANSWER BY LIVING

Einstein didn't speak as a child
waiting till a sentence formed and
emerged full-blown from his head.

I do the thing, he later wrote, which
nature drives me to do. Does a fish
know the water in which he swims?

This came up in conversation
with a man I met by chance,
friend of a friend of a friend,

who passed through town carrying
three specimen boxes of insects
he'd collected in the Grand Canyon—

one for mosquitoes, one for honeybees,
one for butterflies and skippers,
each lined up in row, pinned and labeled,

tiny morphologic differences
revealing how adaptation
happened over time. The deeper down

he hiked, the older the rock
and the younger
the strategy for living in that place.

And in my dining room the universe
found its way into this man
bent on cataloguing each innovation,

though he knows it will all disappear—
the labels, the skippers, the canyon.
We agreed then, the old friends and the new,

that it's wrong to think people are a thing apart
from the whole, as if we'd sprung
from an idea out in space, rather than emerging

from the sequenced larval mess of creation
that binds us with the others,
all playing the endgame of a beautiful planet

that's made us want to name
each thing and try to tell
its story against the vanishing.

SHORT TREATISE ON BIRDS

Adaptation of the Grey-Crowned Rosy Finch
SQUAW VALLEY, CALIFORNIA

Inch by eon they ascended
until higher than trees they found
insects raining onto snowfields
and little to compete with their
feeding on plummeting bounty:
an aerial beltway of bugs
intersecting with peaks, easy
pickings, airlifted, chilled and free.

✳

Flight of the Great Blue Heron
SHEPHERDSTOWN, WEST VIRGINIA

When the great blue heron lifted
from its perch on the Potomac
it flew a long while just inches
from the water's sheen as if the
electrons of its motion could
only flow against that counter-
passage. So, friend, your light stays with
me, though to be light, it goes.

✳

Sacrifice of the White-Winged Dove
TUCSON, ARIZONA

When the ornithologist must
sacrifice white-winged doves to test
for isotopes of saguaro
(he will help the public see that
no species is isolate) he
eats every morsel of flesh. He

wants his body to become, like
theirs, isotopically the land.

❋

Migration of Sandhill Cranes
SULPHUR SPRINGS VALLEY, ARIZONA

Perhaps they would forgive us our
greed if they lived with moral codes.
Instead they take our leavings, corn-
fields crowded with migrants till they
rise, wheel, stream apart in columns
then join again. If they have a
purpose, it must be communal
flight, swarms that meet to read the sky.

❋

Cognition of the Scrub Jay
CAMBRIDGE, ENGLAND

It takes a thief to know a thief,
researchers say, having fed wax
moth larvae (truffles, in jay cui-
sine) to their subjects and finding
the birds understood what other
jays were thinking—when no rival
was looking jays who had stolen
another bird's food would hide theirs.

❋

Lesson of the Spa Sparrows
TUCSON, ARIZONA

We're still so new I can hardly
keep my hands off you while we lounge
in the spa after swimming. A

mother hovers, covering her
daughter with a towel, buds of
breasts sharp inside her suit. Over-
head bold sparrows nesting in the
landscaped shrubs go at it in flight.

✻

Navigation of the Thrush Nightingale
EN ROUTE FROM SWEDEN TO SOUTHERN AFRICA

They don't flock when migrating, each
bird travels by itself, flying
at night and resting by day. When
they reach the Sahara they face
five nights of flying with no food.
First-timers know (tested in lab
simulation) when to feast (hoard
in cells) by reading magnetic fields.

✻

Inspiration of the Peregrine
GRAMERCY PARK, NEW YORK CITY

Wanderer who stood in snowfall
perched on the hoop and stave water
tank over the park—the human
world lost even to us watching
from our ninth floor bed, one white rag—
there!—circling behind the penthouse
glass—you made the city more than
itself, owning the place you landed.

THE CHARTING

Flying to Palermo I watch the dotted red line
plot our course over the Oceano Atlantico,
the Monti Appalachi at our backs, blanks
in the line filling as we leave the continent
and climb into the evening that has already left
Milano but not yet arrived in New York.
Suspended like an instar over Newfoundland,
cabin darkened, passengers disheveled in sleep,
I sip cognac, its heat shimmering in my blood,
and watch a woman sip champagne in the galley,
joking with her husband, charming him with
female vivacity and spangly cardboard glasses,
the eyes two 0s, the 2 and the 1 framing her face.
What time is it here 35,000 feet over the world,
hours after the toasts have been raised in Paris,
hours before they will reach San Francisco,
the turning world always waiting for something,
always getting over something, the same things,
all over the globe. Baby at last asleep, Daddy's
shirttails untucked, my seatmate collapsed over
two seats, blanket over her head—what *was*
that pill she popped as we taxied out of Kennedy?
Sleep. Broken by silent fragments of a film.
Turning. Aching. Synthetic diurnal rhythm
of mechanized flight.

                         I'm a day late because
a blizzard hit New England, snow starting at dawn
and closing the woods around my mother's house.
I shoveled the pathway, hauled wood and watched
the white unfurling—four inches at breakfast,
ten inches at lunch, mid-afternoon and the whiteness
had muffled the world down to the small circle
at the end of my pen. Two storms converged
off the coast, spinning together into a galaxy,
its force canceling everyone's business. Beautiful
to be subdued by its quiet, where I could only think

about flying to Palermo and wonder what my mother
at ninety, not a woman who welcomes help, would do
alone in a blizzard. One day, she said, when the dog
brought home a rotted deer carcass, she whacked
the meat and bones apart with a hammer, bagged
the remains and drove them to the dump. I can feel
her frustration and her strength, bemoaning the dog's
disgusting habit but energized by the task, and if
someone had come along to help her, all she'd have
felt is frustration. That's why she'd rather let the snow
pile deep against the door, while I fly off to—
it doesn't really matter where I've gone.

Palermo now where boats oar out at dawn
past marly cliffs and return filling crates
that line the sidewalk—glittering anchovies,
spiraling periwinkles, black bursting sea urchins,
half-moon steaks of swordfish and whole
octopus, flesh white as porcelain
speckled purple as wine, lifted from the
open-air pot and sliced before my eyes—
oh the beauty of the customer who stands
at the streetside bar to wait, the winter street
spilling conversation like heat from open doors.

I'm here because two hundred years ago
the monk Piazzi discovered the first known
asteroid and named it Ceres. His portrait
honors the muse Urania, science owning up
then to its sisterhood with art. In his observatory
the globe shows North America, in sepia,
unnamed—Indian Territory and Uncharted Land.
I'm here because now the charting continues
in space (how many gravity assists does it take
to fly past the moon?) and an audience
has gathered to hear what poetry has to say
about where we are. An expert reports that
astronomers consider asteroids vermin—
they clutter space between Mars and Jupiter,
streaking the clarity of stars. But really,

the expert adds, we should consider them
friends, places we can use for staging (land there
and mine them) when we go to Mars.

                                    Not my job
to put spin on asteroid reputations, though
they can use it since one slammed to Earth
leaving an iridium spike at the K-T boundary—
global darkness for a year and the shrinkage of dinosaurs
into birds. My job to argue for beauty not use
(see Galileo's washes of the moon; see Kepler's
Somnium; see Nabokov: "I discovered in nature
the nonutilitarian delights that I sought in art").
My job to argue for dark skies that make us see stars
and say where oh night did I come from and
where (coded for long distance) am I going?
My job to be the lepton thoroughfare that is me
and the storm and the stars and the dark matter
that perforates everything with its missingness.
How to feel whole knowing we're shot through
with holes made of the inverse of all we know?
Inherent in matter is something unwounded by puncturing.

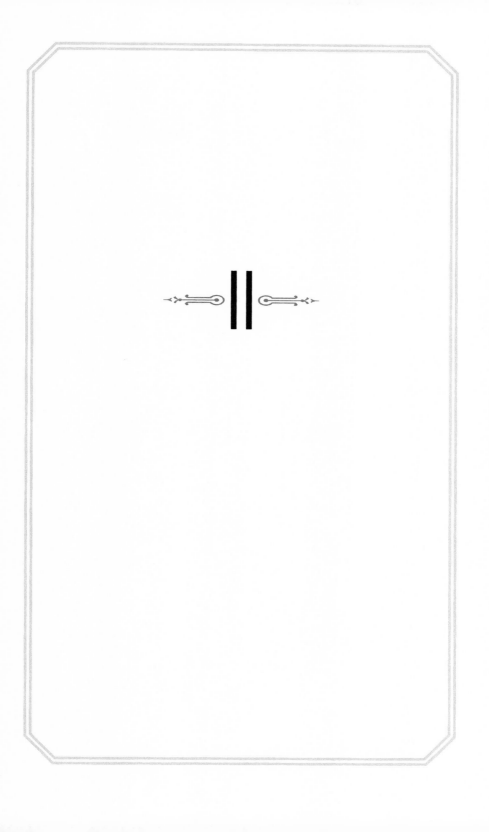

CONSCIOUSNESS ACHIEVING THE FORM OF A CRANE

What if the universe—
whatever impels it to fly
apart and find the force
of attraction—is no
different from my mind that
chooses to leave you to
cook in the kitchen—minced
greens and onions in small
steel bowls, skillet heating
cumin and oil till we're
breathing curried air and
I settle by the far
windows to watch how the
monsoon builds. What if my
leaving expresses my
certain love for you? Would
I differ from stars that
do affinity in
motion or from desert
clouds spilling rain that can't
touch the ground hanging in
streaks mid-sky though water
by its nature has to
cycle back to land and
fit itself to flowing?
Oh my love we are at
home with ourselves at last
and it is peaceful when
I lie pressed all night to
your neighboring skin then
wander alone into
cloud-making weather to
find that when I look out
I see you in the glass
a trick of light that brings

you back to me even
when I think I'm alone.

—after the painting by Morris Graves

UNION SQUARE

Over breakfast in the faux fifties diner
we flip through the jukebox titles, choose
"The Book of Love" and talk about
how the connecting works with us—
how easy it is for you to find yourself
in a place you don't want to be, a model
so rigid the only way out is to break,
and how easy it is for me to feel I can't
do partnering, turn faithless and fall
into myself—then together finding those
hindrances, as with gears when in sync,
are the reason our joining works.

At the rental desk the clerk asks, Are you
husband and wife, and I giggle, Well,
not exactly, and turn my love-happy
face to yours. The woman standing in line
behind us with her man is watching, stiff
and not pleased to be where she is. Later
you guess she's traveling with her boss
who's her lover though that's not what
she wants. She'd like to break the bad contract
she's made with herself. And you imagine
telling her, Forget him, come with us.
We're going to the beach, we have a car.

Rush hour and the urban outflow pours
across the Million Dollar Bridge. I wait
for the walk-light, cross-traffic slight but
caution's the rule when the city roars
toward all its separate homes. I get
the sign, little electric man, and step
into the street. A woman turns into
my lane, bearing down, eye-contact,
and still she guns it until I stare and
shake my head in disbelief at her
ferocity. She slows begrudged to let
me pass, runs down the window of her Saab
and shouts, "Why don't you wait for the light?"
and flips me the bird. I feel weepy like
a punished child, mind sinking to lament,
What's wrong with the human race? Too many
of us, too crowded, too greedy for space—
we're doomed, of course, so I head for coffee
and a muffin, walking sad and slow on
the return. I'm waiting again to cross,
picking fingersful of muffin from the
paper sack and watching the phalanx of
cars race by, not even a cell of a
thought in my mind that I might jump the change,
when a man who's got the green stops,
an executive wearing a crisp white
shirt and shiny red tie, and he raises
his palm to gesture me safely across,
making all the cars behind him wait while
I walk, and together at rush hour that
man and I redeem the whole human race.

WILD FRUIT

But take heed lest by any means this liberty of yours become
a stumbling block to them that are weak.

—Paul, 1 CORINTHIANS 8:9

1

At the cusp when spring begins
to turn into summer, come
the strawberries, little
baby's knuckles,
lying low in the scrub
so that one who would taste
their juice must kneel
or lie on the ground,
testing her gentleness.
Their season is short, yet
if she grows impatient,
she will carry home
only their blood
soaked into the knees
of her jeans. They are so
precious that a woman
might refuse to eat them—
five years worth in jars
untouched on the shelf—
but she would grow bitter
from trying to hold on
to that which will pass.

2

If you want wild raspberries,
level an acre of forest
and leave the lot
a mess of bleaching brush.

The brambles will crawl
out of the rubble
as if to compensate the land
for its grievous loss.
To pick the berries you must walk
knee-deep in deadfalls,
waist-high in thorns, and
compete with yellow jackets.
You must inch your way
into thickets, crushing a path
through the canes, throwing off
the green beetle and white spider
that rise in your bucket like
stones in a farmer's field.

And when you are done,
backtracking through
your own destruction,
you will step free of the uncertain
ground and walk happily, perhaps
through a meadow of ferns,
to come home, lay ice
on the bee stings, and
savor, in small handfuls,
the healing taste of the wild.

3

Most of the blueberry patches are gone—
roads widened, backlots plowed,
ridges claimed. On Beech Hill
they subsist on the skin of soil
covering bedrock, at the summit
stone breaking through like bone
on a wounded elbow. The bushes
lie low, and it is a mystery why
such scrawny plants are not overtaken
by scrub of alder and spruce.
Perhaps their taste for acid ground

is more refined. But where they find
the ingredients to make their version
of the color blue or the flavor
that could remind a monk of sex—
these are questions for which I want no answers.

4

No one but myself to blame
for being late to get the gooseberries.
The only patch unpicked, one growing
over a domestic dump—little patch
of china shards, rusted arcs of tin,
and rotted pillow ticking behind
a place where once a family was—
gnarled now with nettle and rugosa,
the fruit smelling winy and falling
at my touch. But I'm persistent
when it comes to berry picking,
driven by the avarice to know
how even this late and wasting
fruit that guards itself
with row upon row of rigid spines
might serve to make me thankful.

5

The blackberry is like
a person who puts off
saying the thing
she most wants to say
so that finally
the words blurt
too large and clumsy.

The blackberry puts off
making its fruit
until its canes

tower and arc
over those
which have expended
themselves early in summer
and winter is just about
to wrap its hands
around the stalks.

After spending so long
making itself strong
it cannot promise
that its fruit,
gravel seeded,
will always be sweet,
All it can promise
is abundance.

NEW SHOES, 1939

Is that a receipt
or a love note folded
on the open box?
Red suede heels so tall
they force the ankle
to incline, the calf
to tense. Someone wants
to see her legs shout
their form. Are there laces
or buttons that close
the leather around
her, leaving a seam
of white skin asking
for a tongue? To open
them, a man must be
good with his hands, slow
and precise, though they
are not shoes for courtship
but come here and have
me right now shoes, or
shoes for the jitter
bug, strong for hard
dancing, though no one
has worn them so far,
an invitation
only, they pose by
the box, a small stage
where a drama or
comedy could take
place. She has unwrapped
the shoes and now waits
for his call, the man
who will love her for
wearing them. Or he
has called many times,
hoping he has found
the gesture that will
bend her strength to his

desire. Or her will
is the instrument
of desire, the heel
so stout she will not
fall—oh and the world
behind the shoes is
drab, beige table,
brown wall, a fallow
place where shoes become
the dark tulips of
love. Maybe her love
goes only as far
as these shoes—what dance,
what music, but the
struggle for form
that inspires her hand?
Not a shoe for hiking,
for working, not a worn-out
shoe. The Depression
is over and now
she can contemplate
beauty—pure product
of America
planted in a field
of tissue paper
green. No one wears these
shoes and they look best
that way, no scuffs, no
sagging—the poverty
is over and what
will make us great now
is uncertainty,
what opens in the mind
when things do not
reveal a single
meaning, but make us
reach into the invisible.

—after the painting by Katherine Schmidt

THE PHENOMENOLOGY OF SHOPPING

Fax it to me he said and
I said I will though it meant
since I was living in a cabin
on the coast driving to town and
chatting with the innkeeper
for an hour because that is
the neighborly rhythm
of a small town and since
I had already disrupted
the quiet of my day I drove on
to the city to check out
the outlets and buy pasta
and wine—a fine Valpolicella
so cheap I bought three—
and listened on the long drive
home to the radio telling me
how many pounds of dump space
I would save each year
if I used less stuff—comics
for Christmas wrap, mixing
frozen juice in a pitcher
instead of buying it in glass—
and I scanned the bags beside me
that had grown like spores
in the petri dish of my car and
felt as if I'd no hand in their
multiplying and asked myself
in disgust, "Who's driving this car?"

ZOOLOGY

Driving home on the icy interstate
my friend the zoologist tells me
there's not a single nestling
along the eastern shore. They're
just a concept until spring
and it's up to us to keep them

alive as abstractions. It's a lesson
I might tell my students—pretend
the idea matters until it does. A species
becomes extinct unless you remember
the tinsel-scrap and wattled straw
that air-boned vagrant made its home

before nestling became fledgling became
gone. Then you can make it matter
that a kid parks his bicycle
to take his first job, that a refugee
stacks newpapers and thinks of the dead,
that he sings the opera of the country he's lost.

You don't need me to teach you
that nothing's a bargain—you know
the history of loss cuts into each deal.
The only treasure is what you imagine—
the grubby child of your idea,
so frail it throws tantrums to prove it's alive.
But it needs you to love it, to teach it to talk.

—for Bezo Morton

THE OLD MAN

The old man offers to lead me
past the *heiau* to the waterfall,
a public place made private
by the new man's fence and pit bull.

You know that plant? he asks.
Ti, I answer and he laughs,
You smart fo' . . .
He won't say the word that means

I don't belong here, though
my knowing the plant is worth
something in both our minds.
We pluck wild mangos from the trees,

five-finger cherries. Does he know
any stories about this place?
Yes, but he won't tell them.
Scares people and they won't come.

Once on this island there were priests
so powerful they could pray
a person to death. At sixty-nine he
billygoats up rocks and hills, we stave across

the boiling stream that tugs our legs,
climb out into *noni* grove, reeking fruit
he gulps as we walk. Good for heart,
thumping scrawny chest. Are they

commercially grown, I ask. He stares
as if I'm crazy. That could never
happen. They'd all be killed or cut down.
He doesn't say by whom or what, just knows

whatever forces make such a gift
would take it away if improperly used.
After hours in the woods—bird nest
plant, he says, two people could

climb in there and make love—I wonder
what to offer him as payment
for guiding me and I realize
I have nothing he wants.

—for Charlie at Halawa Falls

THE CHANGING PLACE

Not a scheduled stop
but the day is hot
and I can change here
a village moored boats
trimaran anchored
offshore customers
floating with snorkels
watching the bright fish
dart and glide their joy
to watch and mine too
to sit on stones where
a temple once stood
two man-sized fish gods
such plain stone that the
woman who sunbathes
here each day does not
notice them remote
and useless as they
have become what is
the energy of
this place where I am
not out there in the
social sea but here
seeing if in all
things then in me too
that force that holds me
not emptiness but
the presence of things
that cannot be seen.

VOICE

Some nights sleeping in
the rainforest house
where wind made the loudest
noise I woke to song
and could not tell
whether one voice or
two whether from the
house next door or woods
above whether chant
or psalm or keening
I did not want to
ask or admit my
ignorance hearing
something so private
it sounded like a
wail of pain then slipped
into pleasure and
I listened to the
fragments blow in through
the screens until I
drifted back to sleep
head swimming in the
music and reaching
into its darkness
my questions small notes
in the score more rain
tapping on thick leaves

DRIVING THROUGH NATURE

Past the canyon's rosy gouge and spires,
past the whack of copter blades and booked rooms,

past ponderosa and piñon scrub, the shacks begin.
Dirt lot, brush fence, nomad shelters built for shade.

American flags snap on the scrapwood stalls
where the Navajo sell rugs and beads,

behind them, the planet's skin
stretched out bare and raw so that it seems

the land will tell its story to anyone—
rifts and upheaval, wear and rest.

I'm tired of trying to find a place
where history hasn't left its scars and wounded.

There is only one Earth and its laws
are a mystery we're here to solve.

THE ROCK FIG

Drenched in the cascading
song of canyon wrens,
its gray wood spills out of rock
in the driest, most remote
arroyos, like plastic extruded
from a seam in the tuff,
like cables spooling from
a cave, like sheeting drapes
of liquid stone, like tentacles
the tendrils stuck to stone—
inadequate, all the words
and equations that might
describe something as simple
as wood that has responded to
day after day spent in one place.

Some say that its presence
describes the discipline
of water—floods uprooting
all that grows in their
bouldering path—so that
meeting a rock fig means
understanding the interval
between violent events.
Some say its tea can cure
snakebite in mules and cattle.
Some carve their passion
in its bark and decades later
others find it, a new testament
that echoes with the locating
calls of evening bats
off the rosy canyon walls.

—for George Huey

LEAVING THE ISLAND

Out of the cradle of solitude
the rocking vessel carries you
out of the cold rain and stone jetties
the steepled firs lost in fog
out of the meadows of vetch and rue
the wilting buttercups—
it is never easy leaving the island
passing the signs of progress
an old poppy garden
taped off for blading—
it is never easy entering the city
and walking before the cafés
wake up expecting everything
when you want it angry you can't
get breakfast at dawn when
on the island you'd be happy
with rocks birdsong and weeds.

THE GARDEN IN WINTER

After you left town a blizzard pelted
land's end. Gulls could barely fly
falling airborne backward on the gale.

Whatever pattern governed the sky
fell like a seine over town
until cars whispered to a standstill

and the streets shut down. How tame
Commercial Street could sound,
caught in that delicate net, the shops

made docile by the storm. I walked
to your gated garden, fallen snow
pronouncing the spikes of cut annuals,

softening the hedge's brittle skeleton,
and flaunting how the blue Alberta spruce
held its color. "Blue," you said,

"the most difficult of garden colors,"
devoting one arcing brickwalled tier
to its husbandry. Now the deepening cold

covers the bed where they grew,
all the cultivated layers held dormant—
veronica, statice, blue salvia,

and aster—the last flower to be killed by frost.

—for Stanley Kunitz

HOVENWEEP

One narrow box canyon opened in Earth to let the heretics out.
You can't build the ceremonial house above ground!
Theory of Hovenweep: *Los Alamos. Arco Santi.*
Think tank of the Anasazi, towers perched on boulder and
fallen
rimrock, so unified with sandstone the structures look like horn or
antler
growing upward and away from the forehead of the Great
Sage Plain.
Theory of Hovenweep: astronomical observatory, architectural college,
laboratory for students of the drought, fortress and aviary
for macaw
traders who risked the blistering walk from a
thousand miles south.
Where is the place you go when the story you live in doesn't
work?
Theory of Hovenweep: the whole canyon a musical instrument, the whole
canyon
a signaling device, the whole canyon a solar calendar, portals
to make sunlight tell you how to thrive.
Hackberry sprawls in the head-of-canyon seep where the check-dam
once fed
terraces of squash and beans and corn.
Empty granary under sandstone eaves where the clarity of glyphs
recedes from light: handprint, spiral, bird and T-shaped
door.
One narrow box canyon opened in Earth to let the heretics out.

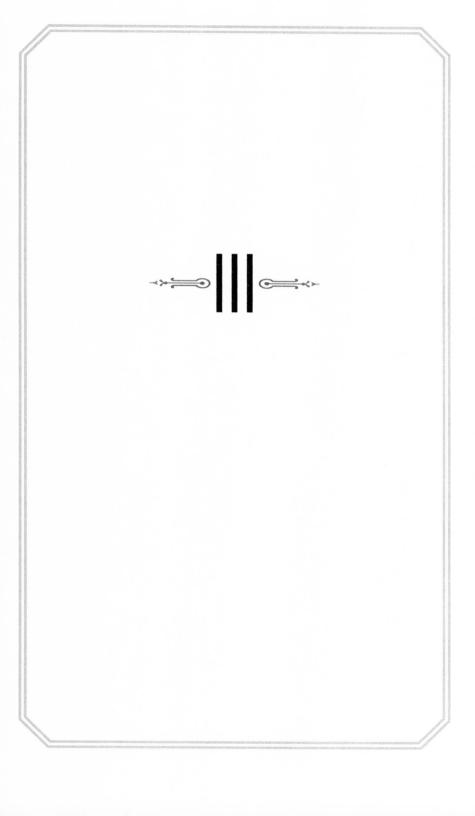

LEARNING AGAIN TO LOVE

First comes love of the world before all else.

—*James Hillman*

I took my loneliness out for a drink
in Prescott, Arizona. It felt female and
embarrassed to drink alone beside
the cowboy hats who watched
the scores and plays on a muted screen
tacked above our heads, Louisiana
blues wailing in the air. The waitress,
hair pulled in a tail as thick and long
as a horse's, thanked me for the tip
with a look that said she knew
who I'd come to entertain and she
was sorry I had to do it alone. I drove
out of town into the national forest,
winding through the darkening pass
toward ferocious scarlet sky. I parked
to watch the blaze die. Gray storm clouds
had stopped their dumping, but clung
to mountain snags like sheep's wool
stuck on burdock. Below, the scrubby
chaparral fell, ravine after ravine,
snow tufting the high points, a little pink
leaking under the ceiling to the west.
Rising from the forest came clicks and distant
isolated shrieks of birds and creatures
I could not name from their voices alone.
Now from the north, now the east, from all
the points that had passed already into dark.
Each wished to know each other's location
as night settled them down, each one
in some protected space. Then a Cadillac
passed by, heading for the switchbacks,
its hum softening to a whir, and I noticed
once again how I love my solitude
in the same way I love the last corner

of sky to hold the day's electric glow.
I thought of driving off into the air
like those women, movie outlaws,
whose only choice was to fly into their own finale,
but no one was chasing me, so I did not.

MAKING LOVE TO YOU WHEN YOU'RE FAR AWAY

Sometimes it starts with words,
like when you're jammed
with work and have no time
and I say to myself, Baby,
there's always time for love,
and you take me then,
miles away and buzzed on
a thousand decisions about
windows or doors or cement,
and I do it myself with you
in mind and it's almost as
sweet as if you were there,
until it's over and you're not.

Sometimes it's a memory, say,
your graceful return that time
I threw something glib at you
and learned how substantial
you could be when I didn't
even know I needed that, but
I did, the way I need it now,
the thing you would give me
that I could not anticipate,
the lack I could not feel
until you replaced it with
something present. I want
to tell you the truth
without scaring you away.

Sometimes I think of love
as a dangerous storm
that makes me hunker down
in a powerless house
beside a flame too small
to keep me warm. I have been
reading the history of my problems
with men for as long as
I have been living it,

looking for the lessons
that would let me graduate
from the hard-knocks school of love—
no more painful requirements to fulfill
once I master the practice.

Today it started right here
on the page, hearing my voice
as if I were Penelope,
past anger, just waiting
and working in the dark, and
I had to leave my desk,
getting lost in you again,
both of us coming to a place
we had never been before,
a place we wanted to stay. What woman
can say she doesn't want
the moment in the myth when
Psyche lights the lamp,
unable to resist any longer
seeing what has been forbidden?

WHAT HAPPENS NEXT

Burned and wounded
he turns from her.
He is a god
and does not know
pain though now he
feels it where the
hot oil of her
lamp has spilled at
the juncture where
his wings begin
to bud and fledge.

PENELOPE ZEN

I want to be the harbor
he sails into
not another storm.

✳

To be constant
I unravel
in solitude
beginning again
unencumbered.

✳

Though friends mock me
or send condolences
it is my practice
as a woman
to love
and by this
to cultivate my self.

✳

Not sacrifice
not compromise
to give away
what I have made
making room for
what I have not.

✳

I want to be
the harbor
not the storm.

LA PAZ

Not that desire stops with celibacy
going into the ache where
your ghost comes on to me
making love in a spectral place
that hums with its own dense music.
I'm thinking too hard because
what I want is to have you and
I can't though the thinking
turns me on—what we say when
the inner life begins again
to buzz with electrons—which is why
I'm inventing you standing
on a balcony in a foreign city
the extremity of a place
whose foreign name means peace—
what I've had none of since that hotel
and now in another alone listening
to secondhand parade music
rise from the street and watching
a spring snow melt as it falls
on the city's gray skin I'm thinking
I don't want to carry the burden
of my solitude another day.

BLACKTAIL

Dusk. The moon a notch past full.
I step out my door to test
the weather, meet a blacktail
walking down the empty street.
We stop and stare. I back off.
She walks carefully on. I step out
and find myself between that one
and another, lame, who follows
with pain, front leg broken at the
shoulder so she can't set the hoof
to ground, her ribs lined stark as bars,
pelt dull and sunken. For months I've seen
their tracks in sand but never known them.

BIOPHILIA

On the day I found the snakemouth orchids,
little explosions of organic joy,
blooming in the spaghnum bog, you were walking

a thousand miles away and found a half-grown
gopher tortoise, head collapsed on dozer-paws,
asleep beside the trail. No dreams to dream,

you wrote, just evolved too soon. And there it lay
in the awful smolder of wildfire and
summer heat, waiting for its mind to change.

But I was dreaming about you, a closeness that distance
didn't erase but underscored. Some days I wonder if
I should trust how quickly my mind has changed

from hermitage to love nest, as if I could explain
the marriage of my solitary ways with the hopes for love
that I still harbor. My birthday today—fifty-two.

Number of cards in the deck, weeks in the year—a completeness
in the number reminds me of the holy ratio mystics quote
to convince skeptics that the universe wants order

and proves its desire in pattern and form. I walked today
across the breakwater—granite blocks that encumber
and gentle the tide—to swim in the reed-lined channel

where I love feeling the gentle tug of planetary
motion, my arms pulling with or against it
in the silky brine. A busload of kids from the city

arrived, parading out along the great stones,
dressed in bright yellow T-shirts that made them
look like daisies blooming for a mile across

the water to Long Point's curl of sand. The girls
screamed at spiderwebs spanning the rocky gaps,
and the boys said, Man, that water feels good.

Last in line came a boy who was stupid or blind or
just incomplete, his senses slow, movements timid,
every step a challenge to the fear that kept him

closed so tightly inside his awkward body
he could not move freely even in the open air
of the beautiful world—sea glittering like fish scales,

marsh grass electric green in sunlight, the gulls
and the children singing cantatas. An older boy
walked the slow one along, instructing him—

Step here, now lift your body up—and listened to the
unfinished words the other spoke, saying back to him
their meaning; patiently, so patiently, one child

led another, just held that hand and looked around
enjoying the day, his kindness bringing him into
the joy of it. "Has anyone known a sorrow like mine?"

asks the old hymn, and everyone knows the answer
is supposed to be, No, until one hears the words
sung to a melody, and a roomful of strangers

begins to weep, at first in sorrow, but then, seeing
others weep, knowing that the answer is, Yes,
and in that sharing the tears mean joy. When you wrote me

about the tortoise—how it lay in a forest that had been
the bottom of an ocean, only the ghosts of fishes for company—
I knew you loved the world's beauty and mystery in a way

that made me love you, and I knew I was finished
waiting for my life to catch up with my art—all that love
dispersed to bog orchid, migrating butterfly and

eucalyptus outgrowing its bark; all that cultivated
wonder at the earth's dizzy recapitulation of the theme
no sorrows can stop; all that paying attention

to the beauty of the small, teaching me it's in our nature
to love, just as it's in the blackberry's woody canes
to bear fruit, in the black-throated green warbler's breast

to sing its repeating song, every mystery
of planet or heart, every longing that ever led you
where you needed to go in spite of your best intentions,

every act of bearing witness, lament or praise, adding up
to knowing that *what* we love—hardwired, generative,
biologic power—could teach us *how* to love,

bright and awake to each other, alive under the surprising sun.

—for Bill

THE LIST

How I took a beach walk for you after hearing
    that the tears had returned and would not stop

How I thought of us sleeping together
    like brother and sister
    in a poor family that hadn't enough beds

How when I slept in your bed, you taking the couch
    in a kind way you made sound like convenience,
    I woke coming in a dream finding your mouth on me

How I thought, disappointed, it's only a dream,
    and then to prove it reached down, still dreaming,
    found your face there and took it in my hands

How then we learned each other's wounded places,
    what is grotesque and what is beautiful

How I thought that to tell you this might violate
    friendship's unspoken covenant

How I told you anyway because a friendship
    ought to taste of the inner life

How I was like the excited child who says—Look,
    look what I found—though by then
    it's always gone and no one else can see it

How I thought of several explanations for your grief
    but knew that each would be useless

How the burnish of the day's ending
    was a little seam of fire
    that stitched the wave to the sky

How I knew the tears would pin you like a specimen onto the page
    and no mere change of circumstance would be sufficient
    to undo your pain

How I thought selfishly if you could not keep
    your hard contract with living then mine would grow harder

How I wanted you to know yourself to be nothing and feel grateful
    because any knowledge is better than oblivion

How I wanted to give you something you would remember
    next time you pass a gunshop and think why not

How I hoped that one or two or three of these things
    might help to keep you alive

—for Simone

ON SAGADAHOC BAY

Mid-tide, when the sandbar floods,
the deeper channel marks a curving path,
dark seam of water where the ocean
enters twice a day to fill the sheltered cove
and swab the land leaving shells and husks
of finished lives along the beach. The land
too does its part, peninsula of pointed firs
that reaches out and leaches salt
into the seminal broth. I'm learning here
to see relationship instead of boundary,
my life as small as an ankle-high wave
that rises only once, say, at high tide
when it can catch the moonlight in its fist,
then curves and falls back into the
complexity that gave it form, energy
released into molecular flow. Each wave
comes only once, but the tide,
being movement, remains itself forever.

THE BEAUTY OF WALLS

The beauty of walls is that they need continuously to be nourished and repaired.

—Andy Goldsworthy

To clear the place   cut down the trees   and make a field
later the only place   left free of work   is the wall
and trees find   protection there   as fields are groomed
and walls forgotten   until someone finds them   collapsed

sheltering the saplings   and the man   who finds
but never owns beauty   remakes the wall   in sympathy
with oak and maple   making the wall loop and lope   around their trunks
until it walks   under the water and across the road   or did it stop there?

The joy I feel   in art these days   is where   I am at home
in the world   sublime and grievous   it is how I know
the soul is real   and that its life   is why I'm here
its windy accretions   its useless meandering   its wind in the trees.

BEAUTY

I found a giant pelican
     standing peg-legged on sand
waves sloshing behind its back
     webbed foot lifted
to ease the pressure
     where a fishhook lodged
filament curling loose
     and tangled underwing
the downy crested head
     bent low, eyes half shut,
the warming sun and trance of waiting,
     its portion of beauty
for this day as meager and real as
     the prisoner's trowel
kept hidden at peril of his life
     because the only
beauty in the gulag
     was the dignity of work.

REHEARSAL SPACE FOR WAR

East of Gila Bend two jets release payloads
that billow the desert dirt, rehearsal space for war

is what the desert means to military minds, a meaning
the civilian mind will never understand, as it walks

through the details of the day: buy bananas, check
bank balance, water plants. There is a god that lives

in the weapons, a power that exists in the mind
capable of imagining that to slaughter people

is a just way to solve injustice. What fool or monster
would instruct children to launch bombs upon the bully

terrorizing a crowded playground? To be a fool or monster
is to believe there is only one way. Avenging genocide

is an expensive means of focusing the mind.
The civilian mind rehearses taking in the wounded,

their faces sinking below the reflective darkness
of public memory, taking in the warriors who will own

forever their elation in battle, the pageantry of war
that comes home and joins the ticker tape parade,

the Disneyland soundstage of victory, a word
that cannot disguise suffering—the smoke and blade

fever of destruction that leaves the living to question,
Was it right, what I did? Was it mine, the choice to quit?

IN THE KAMPINOS FOREST, POLAND, 1940

         matronly the women being led
to the killing site by
                soldiers who guide them

         each man escorting a woman who
might be his mother placing his hand
                on her arm so she will not stumble

         this one wearing a checkered housecoat
watching where she places
                her feet on the leafmold

         as they walk together through saplings
bleached lifeless with light—
                who thinks the forest is a refuge

         from history does not know
history or forests—only the trees
                can turn this ground

GENIUS LOCI

Return

Return to a place where nothing in particular can be seen
        to explain why you return, nothing you can name,
    though you can touch the memory of the landscape—

linden trees in a hedgerow, cut wheat field, ruins of the longhouse,
        rolling meadow of sunflowers blooming, the musk of their oil,
    contained heat. This is the place of the early believers,

where one granite outcrop, one muddy sinkhole, can infect you
        with a memory three million years old—what history
    has done to shape the brain, early bronze people who softened sinew

in the pocket of their cheeks to lash blade to shaft—their rumination
        happening *here* where you stand
    in the lime of snails knowing nothing about your debt to snail or neolith

but that you are called back to lives you never knew,
        into the abstractions that people the mind—not the haploid
    cellular past, but the *beings* of thoughts, real as the realm they inhabit.

✳

River

Rocks have the oldest knowledge on Earth, rivers have
        the oldest names and determine where the cities shall be built
    and what shall be their shape. The Vltava here sinuous and slow

so the city turns and turns back into and against itself,
        streets winding like folds of the brain so that finding your way
    means getting lost—arch, alley, cobblestone—the angels and demons

descended to perch on rooftop and balustrade enjoying the beauty
        and soot that only mortals can construct. The salmon are lost—
    gone half a century (who counts fish when half-track tanks

roll into town?)—but the river still does its work, harboring coots,
      grebes and mute swans, the river keeping its own clock,
   doing its commerce of moving silt and gravel, rafting birds downstream.

✳

       Here the weak die easy as a feather
           And when they die, they die forever.

✳

Horologe

Only the past and present are real,
the future may never arrive
to add more real to the world.

The clock gives the hour, the day,
the month and the year
a place to stand—again the skeleton

tips his hourglass and what was empty
with a gesture is full.
What a joke—bones that boast eternity

while gears and cogs and spheres
take you out of time, mind
spilling in the hour of contemplation

so it might be a day you spend watching
the blue center of heaven
where a tiny goldleaf sun and pearly moon

spin round like diligent plebes
running in metallic order, the geocentric
mistake that stays in our brains,

so that even now no one has ever seen
Earth turn toward the sun in morning and away
from it at night. Still "sunrise" and "sunset" say *we*

are the great quiet eye of the celestial storm,
not just one busy cell spinning and whirling,
wobbling in tipsy uncertainty

through the gigantic body of the unknown.
And so the apostles file round
on the wheeling track followed by Christ

who blesses the crowd. The minstrel
raises his mandolin, the cock flaps its wings and crows,
and then the stained glass portals close.

＊

The Castle

It is as if all of them—archangels, apostles and the crowned and bleeding
    Christ—
are blown in a wind of light, broken glass, and fractured color. God
    presides
over the killing of the holy man, his mother wears the dead body as if she
    were the cross.

I choose Saint George for my patron, the necessary killing of the beast, a
    two-tiered project:
first the sword, raised again and again to pierce reptilian muscle, and then
    the brush and chisel
picked up to sanctify the slaughter, the limbic brain and its attendants—
    serotonin, oxytocin—

turning violence into art. I choose chamber music filling the parlor of
    Lobkowicz Palace—
the first violinist, a thin young man, sandpaper of day-old beard, tuxedo
    trousers shirt tie,
no jacket, he leans into Dvořák's lento, the long narrow bruise on his neck

a flag, I think, his lover has left on explored territory, until I see the stain
    glower too
from the neck of the second violinist, a woman with porcelain tight face
    (though

her features soften when she meets the eyes of the cellist, melody echoing
    between them).

The instrument has wounded them, its gently warped edge, the lover to
    which they've bared
their necks. I choose lunch with the Hollywood makeup artist, a student in
    my class,
and we sit in the sun of the Poet's Café eating red cabbage, lentils,
    crumpled sheep cheese,

then strudel (a life of lists—nothing ever complete—yes, there was
    Turkish coffee, maybe white
beans and tomatoes), and we gossip about the bad behavior of the stars—
    the sex goddess
stepping from her trailer—*Is anyone going to get me my fucking cappuccino?*—
    because we love

to know the artifice behind the art, as if any salt-mouthed hardass broad
    could become
the cultivated field where a god would want to plant his seed. *I can make a
    great black eye,*
my lunchmate boasts, *I can do stitches,* her eyebrows sculpted sharp as a
    blackbird's wing.

✳

> *When a new child comes*
> *Everything seems strange to him.*
> *What, on the ground, I have to lie?*
> *Eat black potatoes? No, not I.*

✳

Assembly of the Gods at Olympus

Is that Zeus with the muscular swan draped over his lap, the god lounging
and gorgeous, eyes downcast, one hard nipple protruding against the carpet
of the swan's plumage? He is leaving the human body to become the swan,
his sex already rising as the bird's thick neck, and just at this moment before

the change is complete he can stroke himself as the exotic other. Or, he cannot change back to the man he was, having inflicted that borrowed body—grace used as a weapon—upon his unwilling lover. They are sad, idle and fleshy gods, the dozen who retire in a placeless place, exiled here to settle their disputes in languorous debate, while the doves rub bills, baby angels spill flowers, and Pan with his animal sharp eyes stares down the viewer who would judge them (he knows what you want is lust and delight, then nothing to do but sunbathe). All have their genitals draped in modesty, except Cupid, his childish prick forever innocent. Not one of them can see the stampeding horses, golden fire struck with their hooves as they thunder from the hollows within the gods' mountain retreat, light streaming from its nest in opaque stone, the force of what's to come propelling the animal into the open.

*

Village

I almost miss the bus, waking up in seedy Kajatanka dorm with the maid
    knocking to deliver
two tiny sandpaper towels, taking deathwish elevator to the lobby for
    vending machine
cappuccino thin as broth, stepping outside to sip and—everyone's onboard
    but me.

I race back up for gear, return and climb aboard, maverick blundering into
    the tourist herd.
Is there a tour of underground Prague? someone asks our guide. *Sure,* he
    replies.
But it's illegal. Everything's illegal, but you can do it. Past the city, past cut
    wheat fields

and swirly acres of yellow-headed sunflowers, down the lane lined with
    dwarf apples,
into a nested valley where the Romanesque church stands *almost untouched—*
except big blue hardware store padlock on its iron studded doors—*since the
    twelfth century,*

sooty stone, a weed-grown yard where pedestaled angels lean toward
    ruin.

Since communism fell, the priest makes rounds of a dozen village
       churches, each one
open only every so often. During the regime they stayed open. The secret

police became priests, atheists became seminarians, *the best priests we've had,*
anti-religious propaganda so ridiculous it attracted people to church.
Once the risen breasts and pelvis of a woman were sacred, reverence cut

in stone exalting her form. We're standing near their settlement, the church
laid like river silt over the older faith. In the churchyard's knee-high grass,
someone stumbles on a gravestone—Americans so unaccustomed to the dead

we grow stiff as statues and look around for someone to tell us
what to do, our need so transparent, the guide reassures:
You can really feel the genius loci here. We're standing on generations.

The dead used to be buried inside churches so that to enter you walked on them.
It's the correct position to be standing on dead people. Minutes later:
Funny thing about the postmodern time—now we will be driving past an ostrich
       farm.

*

Ossuary

Is it perversion or sacrament, this chapel
dressed with human bones? When Rome
banned disposal of skeletons above ground,
sacred earth from Jerusalem was scattered
in the village churchyard and everyone wanted
to be buried there; then came the Plague,
so many afflicted the dead were dug up
to make room for more—40,000 sets of bones
exhumed and piled in the monastery cellar
fulfilling the letter if not the spirit of the law;
two centuries later a half-blind monk
stacked the bones in pyramids (something
formal, at least, to honor the memory
that each set once housed a soul); three more

centuries and a carpenter versed in cabbala
felt "the breath of bones"—the endless final
exhalation that calls the living to the dead—
and assembled feeling into form—chalice,
monstrance, garland, and chandelier, gracious
as crystal, containing every bone of the human body,
a craftsman's hand, an eye for beauty, arranging
the fan of scalloped scapulae, cornice of femurs,
candle sconce of skulls each mounted on a tibia,
family crest constructed from ulnae and radii,
dozens in a row, metatarsi and phalanges,
lined in columns, border of ball joints,
and—the victor's boast—skull of the Turk
slaughtered in the Battle of Belgrade
depicted with a raven plucking
the hole where once there was an eye.

*

Hey, try to open up your heart
To beauty; go to the woods someday
And weave a wreath of memory there.

*

Growing into the Tree of the Brethren

A man steps into a chestnut tree as if entering a cave. The bark opens and he
embraces the wood that engulfs him, though his face is turned back
toward the city. He is wild, swept in the winds of passion to be part
of both worlds—the singing in the tavern and the singing in the trees.
He is like an insect stuck in amber, doomed and golden, his last sure
    gesture—
to open his mouth and make the sound he finds there before the quiet hits.

*

Beauty

A corridor of leather-bound books whitened with age.

Catalogued cribs of exotic bugs, shells and desiccated fish.

Mozart's improvised organ sonata, the monk transcribing shards.

Motto of the Premonstratensian Order: What man gains, he passes on.

Locked cupboards for *libri prohibiti*, the work of heretics, preserved.

Green George carries Death out of the Bohemian village and carries
    summer in.

Where of old they sacrificed cattle to demons, let them come on the saint's
    day to eat.

Oh where is Saint George, where is he Oh? He's out in his longboat, all on
    the salt sea Oh!

✳

The holiness of the suffering, which is none of my business.
The loveliness of air, which day after day
Smells of strangeness and carbolic.

✳

Tycho Brahe's Nose

Among the armillary spheres and astrolabes
he directed teams of scholars to measure,
each night at midnight, the exact location
of stars and planets, seeing in motion
something sure and steady, as counterweight
to the mutability of fate—constant wars,
constant plagues, would-be sages selling
turpeth and rhubarbe-hemodactyl, emperor
demanding horoscopes that the Dane refused to give,

while the swarm of soothsayers saw only
profit in the patterns of celestial presence,
not the mystery that sent his longing out
beyond the earthly night to seek
the material of nature—one thing ever
transforming into another, the regularity
of stellar movement sticking to the pattern-
seeking motion of his mind. He had no telescope
and his theory was wrong—sun circling Earth
while all the other planets toed the heliocentric
line. By then he'd already lost his nose in a duel,
the silver and gold prosthesis stuck to his face
with a salve. Kepler inherited his numbers
and used them to find the laws of planetary
motion. But the seeing—that was Tycho's gift—
the metallic shimmer constantly before his eyes.

❋

But in the ghetto darkness too is kind
To weary eyes which all day long
Have had to watch.

❋

Terezín

At first the ashes were placed in a wooden box. Later paper. Always a name
on the box, always notations in the log—how much oil used, temperature
and duration of the fire, name of the shift-workers, cause of death. Four
ovens. Five bodies burned at one time, twenty bodies each twenty minutes.
Not a death camp, just a town for concentrating people who were hated,
sufficient disease, torture, bullets that prisoners hoisted pulley and winch
all night long, sorting collective ash into separate piles, assigning one of
five names. Fifteen thousand children (a life of lists—nothing ever com-
plete) passed through Terezín; one hundred survived. The children at-
tended secret school in the attics—three or six months, one or two years,
depending on their luck. They studied literature and scripture, performed
operas and plays, edited a journal, while the transports arrived and
departed continually. Near the end, covering tracks, the Nazis made a

chain of children (the lucky ones who'd survived) spanning from the crematorium to the river. One night 22,000 urns were emptied into the flow, the pasty sludge dispersing, raining down over carp and crayfish, settling onto the silt where it remains, what hasn't floated downstream with crumbs of bone too light to sink. How many rivers carry such a burden, their music, the psalm: *my sorrow is continually before me.*

✳

Mother, cherish your child, I am a leaf ripe for falling.
See how I cower here, shivering, I am so cold.

✳

Worship

God sits in the light above the clouds,
the angels fly nearby or play lyres or tumble
out of heaven like a storm down toward
the darker world where we live. They seem
more interested in each other than in God.
No wonder there's never been faith
strong enough to protect us from evil
when the divine messengers themselves
are so easily distracted. Or is faith
the child of evil, the mere idea of
transcendence, a necessity to our lives?
Dear ancient gods that sing in the brain
of mockingbird and thrush, that bloom in the
spires of escaped wheat and oregano, that
fatten in the flesh of eye-sized plums, tell me
how do we find our goodness? I stood long
at the gates of the cathedral, the chanting
of monks leaking out, the evening light
angling in to illuminate the golden icons.
On every lintel, cornice, doorframe, column,
niche, some winged or crowned or round-
bellied deity watching over our lives,
protector and admonisher of what we've made.

I followed the worshipers, knowing
the space was made not for those
who stand outside the doors.
I wanted to hear the bones of the organ
and throats of the monks fill the cavernous
vault. I wanted to see—didn't know this until
I'd seen it—each worshiper approach a table
beneath the altar and lift from a small bowl
a spoon filled with salt, pour the white grains
into a smaller bowl, return the spoon to the first vessel
refilling it with salt for the next worshiper,
each person who entered the sanctuary
helping one who follows to be relieved of sorrow.

IN SPRING: DRIFT CREEK

Walking into the hemlock forest,
a place where men years ago had left
their work of notching platforms
into giant trunks where they stood
in teams to saw, we found
soft hulks of long-dead timber
rotting back into the earth
with a fragrance honest as rain.
We found oyster mushrooms and peeled them
from the licheny bark of alders.
It was a place where beavers
had changed the way water moves
over land, where an otter
drew a gentle whirl on the pond's canvas,
where elk had left the imprint
of their strength in the duff.
We were still there when the rain
began, freckling the standing water and
making the young skunk cabbage leaves
shine as if at the opening of a new world.
And now I am holding that stillness
to give it back to you, because the truth is
so much of the world is broken
and I want to be part of its healing.

NOTES

I heard the Latin phrase *genius loci* used casually during my time in Prague and found it preferable to the English equivalent, "spirit of place." The Latin holds an echo of the pagan meaning of the word *genius*—the guardian spirit assigned at birth to a person, place, or institution.

The italicized sections of the poem are excerpts of poems written by children who lived in the Terezín (or Theresienstadt) ghetto, a former garrison town in North Bohemia used by the Nazis to concentrate Jews prior to transporting them to extermination camps. The poems were published in *I Have Not Seen a Butterfly around Here* (Prague: Jewish Museum, 1993).

"Assembly of the Gods at Olympus" is a response to the picture painted by Peter Paul Rubens in 1602. It is on exhibit in the Prague Castle Gallery.

"Ossuary" responds to the bone chapel at Sedlec, the former Cistercian monastery built in 1280.

"Growing into the Tree of the Brethren" responds to a sculpture by Frantisek Bilek (1872–1941) exhibited at his atelier in Prague.

"Beauty" finds its images in the Strahov Monastery library and recalls a passage from Gregory the Great, found in Bede's *History*, as quoted by Bob Stewart in *Where Is Saint George: Pagan Imagery in English Folksong* (Bradford-on-Avon, Wiltshire, England: Moonraker Press, 1977).

"Tycho Brahe's Nose" relies upon two extremely contradictory historical renderings of Prague: the fanciful Angelo Maria Ripellino's *Magic Prague*, translated by David Newton Marinelli (New York: Macmillan, 1994), and the reasonable Peter Demetz's *Prague in Black and Gold* (New York: Penguin, 1997). Brahe worked in Prague under the sponsorship of Rudolph II, Holy Roman emperor (1576–1612) and king of Bohemia (1575–1611).

"Worship" is set at the Abbey Church of the Assumption of the Virgin Mary, Strahov Monastery of the Premonstratensian Order in Prague.

Alden Borders

Alison Hawthorne Deming was born and grew up in Connecticut. She is the author of two collections of poetry, *Science and Other Poems* (1994, winner of the Walt Whitman Award) and *The Monarchs: A Poem Sequence* (1997). Her works of nonfiction include *Temporary Homelands, The Edges of the Civilized World: A Journey in Nature and Culture* (a finalist for the PEN Center USA/West Award for Creative Nonfiction), and *Writing the Sacred into the Real.* She was the editor of *Poetry of the American West: A Columbia Anthology*, and co-edited with Lauret E. Savoy *The Colors of Nature: Essays on Culture, Identity, and the Natural World.* Deming was a recipient of a Stegner Fellowship from Stanford University and has won two fellowships from the National Endowment for the Arts. Her poems have appeared in *Sierra, Orion, The Georgia Review*, and many other publications and anthologies. She currently is Professor in Creative Writing at the University of Arizona and lives in Tucson.

PENGUIN POETS

TED BERRIGAN
Selected Poems
The Sonnets

PHILIP BOOTH
Lifelines

JIM CARROLL
Fear of Dreaming
Void of Course

CARL DENNIS
New and Selected Poems,
*   1974–2004*
Practical Gods

BARBARA CULLY
Desire Reclining

ALISON
HAWTHORNE
DEMING
Genius Loci

DIANE DI PRIMA
Loba

STUART DISCHELL
Dig Safe

STEPHEN DOBYNS
Mystery, So Long
Pallbearers Envying the One
*   Who Rides*
The Porcupine's Kisses

ROGER FANNING
Homesick

AMY GERSTLER
Crown of Weeds
Ghost Girl
Medicine
Nerve Storm

DEBORA GREGER
Desert Fathers, Uranium
*   Daughters*
God
Western Art

ROBERT HUNTER
Sentinel

BARBARA JORDAN
Trace Elements

MARY KARR
Viper Rum

JACK KEROUAC
Book of Blues
Book of Haikus

JOANNE KYGER
As Ever

ANN LAUTERBACH
Hum
If in Time
On a Stair

PHYLLIS LEVIN
Mercury

WILLIAM LOGAN
Macbeth in Venice
Night Battle
Vain Empires

DEREK MAHON
Selected Poems

MICHAEL MCCLURE
Huge Dreams: San Francisco
*   and Beat Poems*

CAROL MUSKE
An Octave Above Thunder

ALICE NOTLEY
The Descent of Alette
Disobedience
Mysteries of Small Houses

LAWRENCE RAAB
The Probable World
Visible Signs

PATTIANN ROGERS
Generations

STEPHANIE
STRICKLAND
V

ANNE WALDMAN
Kill or Cure
Marriage: A Sentence
Structure of the World
*   Compared to a Bubble*

JAMES WELCH
Riding the Earthboy 40

PHILIP WHALEN
Overtime: Selected Poems

ROBERT WRIGLEY
Lives of the Animals
Reign of Snakes

JOHN YAU
Borrowed Love Poems